A Good Time Ago

Robert Grindal

ALSO BY ROBERT GRINDAL

No Ordinary Day

Published by Dolman Scott Ltd in 2018

'A Good Time Ago'©Robert Grindal 2018

Design and typesetting by Dolman Scott

ISBN: 978-1-911412-64-9

Dolman Scott Ltd
www.dolmanscott.co.uk

To Daisy and Joe
and
in memory of my twin brother Peter

Contents

Acknowledgements

I am especially grateful to Nigel Butcher for supporting my words with his fine illustrations and for his 'Major Pulling Power' cover picture.

My thanks go to Jill, my wife, for proof-reading.

I am again grateful to Frikkie van Zyl and others who have encouraged me, en route to this second publication.

Pony Tale

The pony materialised in 1948 when we boys were five. It lived in the orchard, immediately in front and below White Stacks raised lawn. Beyond the orchard was the rest of the farmland.

Our Uncle John (father's brother and a bachelor) was an architect and had planned and built the house in the late 1930's and both the house design and interior was art-deco and very stylish.

Gran lived with Uncle John in White Stacks, which was just beyond our farm garden. The outlook was a delight for Gran as she could keep an eye on the action across the fields; especially the dairy herd being rounded up early morning and mid-afternoon for milking and us boys would wave to her through her kitchen window from across the fields.

When we were small we had to be wary of the three geese and a gander that father kept as guard dogs. We had a Collie and a Scottie as well but the geese were much more effective. They had free range of the Home Field and farm yard and failed hopelessly to differentiate between friend and foe.

It was wise for us children to have a good idea just where they were.

In the early autumn when the cattle were still out during the daytime, the area around the gateway into the cowshed yard would get not only well poached but boggy, and it would take us boys some time to negotiate our way through it.

However the geese had no such problem and on several occasions I would appear back at the farmhouse in a rare state having left my wellingtons anchored in the mud, giving the lame excuse that they couldn't keep up with me.

So Gran would get some entertainment value from such encounters but she also had the more dubious pleasure of overlooking our pony. It didn't have a proper name which was a bit sad but then it was a rather sad pony.

It was hugely overweight and although Thelwell's cartoon pictures didn't arrive till some years later, pony could well have been the blue-print for his 'little' fat friend.

Evidently pony hadn't been introduced to rationing. To the rest of us in those days obesity was a phenomenon and Pete and I had hardly an ounce of spare flesh on us. Watching

Nan spread butter on bread and then proceed to scrape off more than she put on was something to inspire wonder.

Whilst it made sense in our eyes to have a pony, just why we had been volunteered for ballet lessons was somewhat bewildering. I couldn't imagine who might have suggested that this was a good idea.

Pete and I were delivered to Mrs Pattison's Dancing School, off the Binley Road on the outskirts of Coventry for an hour each week but I can't recall just what we did there. Perhaps my mind going uncharacteristically blank on this topic is just a form of protection.

However I do remember performing at the Coventry Hippodrome when we were about six. There was a production of the Grand Old Duke of York and the ballet schools throughout the city had presumably been scoured to find as many soldiers as possible.

So we two had been press-ganged into the ranks. Of course ten thousand was out of the question; so 60 of us dressed in red uniforms and shako caps were required to march in single file across the front of the stage and then race back behind the backdrop to re-join the file of troops coming back on.

We continued round and around for some considerable time and I supposed we were giving a convincing impression of an army. This impression however was somewhat diminished by the soldier two in front of me. He was unfortunately not fully fit and the running backstage was taking its toll.

He had, over several circuits, developed a severe limp, inadvertently drawing attention to himself.

A loud cry from the audience of 'Come on Hoppy, only one more lap' seemed a touch insensitive.

But getting back to pony; it's similarity to the later Thelwell's version didn't extend to it breaking into anything approaching a trot. On a good day a slow amble was its top speed. It had free-range of the grass in the orchard, if it felt up to the effort of travelling, and presumably ate all the wind-falls that were available.

For accommodation it had an oval-topped corrugated tin shed that I believe was a metal section of an Anderson fall-out shelter and hardly seemed large enough to stable its lodger.

I considered at the time that it was within a whisker of eating its way out of house and home; just a shade broader and he'd never make it through the door!

Once inside it could evidently turn itself round as I'd never witnessed him having to reverse out.

I suppose Peter and I should have felt ourselves fortunate to have pony but our rides were hardly exciting. Often it would refuse to move unless it was on a lead and then it often developed into a battle of wills more resembling a tug of war.

After we outgrew pony, which is obviously a misnomer, father discussed the possibility of acquiring a proper horse but by this time our interest in the species had severely waned. I did ask if a full sized version was an option but I was being over-optimistic.

Father, Nan and us boys would always visit the local Walsgrave Show where we would meet our cousins, John and Alastair, and have the freedom to roam even when we were very young.

I admired the pony racing and pony musical chairs competitions often to 'sweet 16 goes to church just to see the boys'.

It was a revelation to find that not all horses were stubborn and overweight.

But my interest in horses was not really stimulated until my introduction to point-to-point meetings. Horses from the local hunts would be entered into the races and it would be both a splendid social event where we would meet our friends and farming neighbours as well as an opportunity to invest a few bob (shillings in old money). It was always possible to find a friend to put it on the bookies or Tote for you when we were obviously under-age.

Everyone would arrive in their vehicles. The entrance fee was so much per vehicle however many it held and most took a picnic which could be consumed whilst viewing the racing.

We would always know a few of the horses and riders as some would be your farming neighbours and members of the local hunt that would periodically cross your fields trying to maintain contact with the hounds.

At the start of each day's hunting, the hounds, huntsmen and followers, both mounted and those in vehicles would meet at a pre-arranged destination, often near a village pub. From there, perhaps after a swift tipple, they would set out to pick up a scent and then proceed in whichever direction that took them.

The followers in vehicles would note the direction initially taken and then guestimate where that might take them.

Motorised followers would then set off along the roads to a position where they might intercept the chase. This was always a chancy business with the possibility you might not catch sight of them again all day.

I recall making a good guess on one occasion – I saw the hounds far ahead of the mounted followers leaping into a river and splashing their way across. I figured by doing so they'd lost the scent and I wandered across to the near-side bank to see where they might be heading.

But I could hear the recall horn being sounded in the far distance by one of the huntsmen. If the hounds were getting too near to main roads or any other potential hazard they had to be recalled for everyone's safety.

The hounds, milling about on the far bank picked up the recall signal and started to leap back down the far bank into the wide stream and began making their way back across.

The near side bank was very steep and some of the hounds were having difficulty negotiating it. One was having particular problems and I scrambled down the bank aiming to give it a hand up.

In no time it saw its opportunity and using me much like a ladder extricated itself. I clambered out thoroughly plastered and wandered back towards the nearby gate.

One of the huntsmen had arrived and I opened the gate for him to ride through. He gruffly demanded 'Have you counted them?'

Well, as it happened I had made a rough count. 'I reckon about twenty-seven' I replied.

He looked down at me in my bedraggled state in seeming distain and growled 'Thirteen and a half pairs, Boy'.

I stood corrected but thought that perhaps next time he'd have to get down from his 'high' horse and open his own gate.

Mike Ings, of similar age to me and part of a keen hunting family, farmed nearby. He and his sister were regular riders at the local Clifton point-to-point and a horse named Dunsmore Lass was one of their more successful mares.

By fortunate coincidence we were part of the same 2 year National Diploma in Agriculture course when we later attended Shuttleworth Agricultural College in Bedfordshire.

Whilst there, following our interest in National Hunt racing we invested in the 'Sporting Life' on a reasonably regular basis.

Four of us students shared the cost of the daily publication and it had to be circulated between us; so strict allocation periods needed to be agreed.

These periods were divided into the first two lectures of the day, the second two, lunchtime and early afternoon and the system was working well.

Until one day during a farm machinery lecture, disaster struck.

Graham, a fellow joint-subscriber, was deeply engrossed in his broad-sheet which overhung his desk when his next-door neighbour set alight to it. I looked round at the ensuing commotion.

Graham, enveloped in smoke and floating paper ash, was desperately trying to quell the flames.

This incident led, not only to much restricted allocation periods, but a severe caution from our esteemed Principal, Ken Russell. Graham was advised to 'spend much more of your time studying the prescribed subjects my boy and less time studying form.'

More recently our interest in National Hunt racing, encouraged me and son, David, to venture into part ownership of a racehorse. Of course we were never under the illusion that our modest portion of a Chaser would be a sound investment.

However the occasional morning visits to Nigel Twiston-Davies's Naunton stables to see The Drunkenmonkey (yes, its real name) and later Ballybro being exercised on the gallops with the other strings of horses was a wonderful spectacle.

Fergal O'Brien, the 'then' head lad, and now a successful trainer in his own right, always found time to give us updates and show us around the stables, introducing us to some of their more celebrated and successful animals.

These occasions were as enjoyable as the excitement of seeing our horse race and well worth the limited outlay.

I'm only thankful that Pony didn't disenchant me entirely.

A Square Deal

The 7 acre field adjacent to the Home Field was owned by Captain Richard Oliver-Bellasis and his family who lived next door in Shilton House. He was the Squire and his wife ran various village events including the annual village fete. This was always a popular occasion when the locals descended on the impressive house and gardens which included their very own 5 foot high box-hedged maze, though their grass tennis court was strictly out-of-bounds.

Many years later I was to 'inherit' their Victorian mechanical rain-gauge and a number of their gardening tools including a wooden garden dibber engraved neatly with R O B which I still use. The initials stood for Richard Oliver-Bellasis but after her husbands' time his wife, who had always been very kind to us children over the years, thought I'd make a suitable recipient.

Father rented the 7 acres on a long-term basis but there were certain conditions attached:

(i) It must remain a grass meadow and not be cultivated.

(ii) A section approximately 30 yards square in its centre was to be fenced off to protect it from grazing cattle.

Ever since Shilton had its own cricket team they had permission from the Oliver-Bellasis family to use this field for their fortnightly matches throughout the summer.

The Field had one distinct advantage in that the nearest building to the cricket square was the Shilton Arms and the pub garden adjoined the field.

There was a convenient south-west facing grass bank that dropped down from the beer garden to the field on which spectators could relax and view the game often in the afternoon and early evening sun.

It was an ideal setting.

Father was ever mindful of the niceties of the game of cricket and endeavoured to keep animals out of the field for the two days prior to each match. This encouraged any deposits in the outfield to partially dry out and also prevented entirely any 'fresh deliveries'.

Of course the somewhat soiled outfield did add an extra dimension to the game; and whilst this potential minefield was readily accepted as a natural hazard by the home team, it came as an unexpected surprise to most visitors.

The teams and their supporters would meet at the pub to prepare themselves before the game, would break for tea and further refreshments again in the beer garden and then wind up the day there, afterwards. It seemed an ideal arrangement that suited all concerned and many considered winning the match of diminishing importance as the day progressed.

As three, four and five year olds, Nan would walk us round through the fields and we'd join the rest of the spectators on the bank and spend much of the time rolling down it with the other village children.

Other than being a perfect venue for the players the Cricket Field was only one narrow field away from the busy London and North Western Railway Line that ran from London Euston to Birmingham, Manchester and on up to Carlisle, and here at Shilton it ran on a high embankment alongside the Oxford canal for a long section.

Father would always maintain that if you could hear the trains in the farmhouse at night it was going to rain and if you couldn't it was raining. I believed Dad's various profound weather predictions in those days!

The raised rail-track gave us a wonderful view of the express trains that travelled at speed on this level and straight section of line. The more ponderous goods engines hauled a wide selection of our Hornby 'O' gauge rolling stock and with a prevailing brisk wind from the west the billowing smoke and steam, belching from the engine smokestacks, would roll down the embankment and drift across the Cricket Field.

The combination of semi-inebriated players, contaminated outfield and intermittent thick fog rolling across from frequently passing trains added considerably to the supporters' entertainment.

Without these 'local influences' it is probable Shilton cricket would have attracted little or no interest, and any vague memories disappeared, much like the pitch, into the mists of time.

The Cricket Field had other non-agricultural attractions; in the autumn it produced a prodigious quantity of mushrooms and later, when snow was on the ground, was an ideal area for sledging. Dad would tie a long rope from the tractor to the 'ex-army' Shackleton type sledge and tow us at high speed whilst we hung on tight.

But the early to mid 1950's was a time of change; Shilton House was sold following the death of Mrs Oliver-Bellasis and Father purchased the Cricket Field, the orchard and rick yard with its adjoining bomb shelter, to add on to the farm.

Soon after this, a new sports field and changing rooms were constructed to the north side of the village. The cricket team moved out, some reluctantly, from the Shilton Arms to their new abstemious facilities, free from any extraneous matter, smoke and steam.

And our dairy herd now had free range of the previously long protected and sacred turf.

Nan

Nan appeared in our lives evidently when we were about 10 months old.

Immediately following our birth, when our mother died, nurses, friends and relations helped father look after us until he was able to arrange a more permanent solution.

Nan proved to be that solution and became a big part of our lives. To Peter and I it seemed like a normal family relationship, as in those early days we weren't aware that Nan was employed to look after us. She was accepted into our family by all our relations without exception.

It was an idyllic home life for me and Pete, up until we were about 9 years of age when we sensed a slight change in the domestic atmosphere. At first it was hardly evident to us but as the months passed it became gradually more tangible.

Some nights, after we had gone to bed, we could hear the raised voices of father and Nan in discussion immediately below us in the farm kitchen. I would get out of bed to put my ear to the floorboards to try to hear what was going on but found it difficult to draw any conclusion.

The following year when father took us on holiday to Barmouth, without Nan, it started to become clearer. This was the first occasion Nan had not been with us on our holidays. Several evenings during that week we accompanied Dad on the long walk to the end of the promenade.

This had happened of course on previous holidays here but this week there was a difference; he was accompanied by a lady who we were to refer to as Auntie Mary.

It seemed to us that, by coincidence, she and her mother were on holiday in the hotel next door.

It was only then that we started to make a connection between the raised voice discussions, this holiday coincidence and then later liaisons, that we felt our lives were about to change; and we feared not for the better.

We were finding it difficult to relate to our new Auntie Mary and there appeared to be little effort on her part to bridge the gap.

In 1954 when Pete and I were 11, father got married to 'Auntie Mary' and Nan departed. She never again visited our home and it was an extremely sad time for us.

But we were away weekly boarding at Coventry Preparatory School and there was an opportunity to meet up with Nan for a short time on Wednesday afternoons. This occurred on about four occasions when we met in the Memorial Park just across the road from the school.

When Father realised these liaisons were taking place they were forbidden as he believed they were preventing us boys from bonding with our new step-mother.

Whilst this was a sad parting for us it must have been heartrending for Nan.

It was to be over twenty-five years later when I discovered an auntie knew of Nan's address and I wrote to Nan in Rugby where she lived with her sister. I arranged to visit her with my wife, Jill, and our children David and Rachel. It was a happy reunion.

We visited her on a couple more occasions before she died.

I let no-one know I was going to attend her funeral and no-one there would have recognised me but when Nan's friends and relations realised how I had fitted into her past I was welcomed with open arms.

Nan had probably never stopped talking to them about 'the twins' since our reunion.

Reverend Swallow

'That's your Dad's car.'

How could they tell? It was so far away and surrounded by police and other vehicles.

I'd just come out of the classroom at the village school into the playground to find a group of other six year olds gathered and looking along the A46 going out from Shilton towards Coventry.

It was a long gentle incline until it reached the crest then descended more steeply towards Ansty and the Oxford Canal. Dad had some land and livestock beyond Ansty and drove out there either on the tractor or in the Ford Pilot each day.

I peered out into the distance. No, it couldn't be. 'That's your Dad's V8 Pilot' the lad insisted. Perhaps it was and I was just not willing to accept the possibility.

Nan came to meet me and Pete at school and confirmed our fears. A loaded 'London Brick' lorry overtaking another had collided with father's car on the crest.

Although friends and relations were trying not to show their concerns, for our sakes, we were desperately worried.

He was in hospital for three or four weeks followed by a long convalescence at home but made a good recovery.

Neighbouring farmers helped out during this time covering the essential jobs on the farm.

It was no surprise that the car was a write-off. But no sooner was he up and about than he drove into the farmyard in a 2nd hand silver Sunbeam Talbot with large headlights and a pair of trumpet shaped horns. We boys were impressed and excited.

However what we weren't so impressed about was our imminent move to weekly boarding at our new school – the Coventry Preparatory School (CPS). Although there were the two of us, being away from home and the farm for a whole 5 days each week would come as a bit of a shock to the system.

There was much to learn that first week.

The Headmaster, the Reverend Kenelm Swallow was a distinctive gentleman, very tall, thin, and a severe disciplinarian.

In the First World War he'd served as a chaplain in the 2nd Battalion South Wales Borderers. He was present at the Ypres Salient and the Somme and his brother was to die there. He remained with his men at the front throughout that period.

He got in touch with the families of men who died in his battalion and the paternal care he exhibited then made him want to start a school once the war was over.

And so he founded Coventry Preparatory School in 1920.

He was strict, disciplined and obviously religious, and in many ways ran the school along military lines.

His 1st Lieutenant was Miss Gray, the matron. She was a gruff, well-rounded woman, grey by name and nature and on the occasions she spoke it was to complain. She ran the kitchen, fed us sparsely, was in charge of the domestic staff and controlled the boarders (23 of us) all with a rod of iron. Any health issues and we had to report to her though most of us would prefer to endure considerable discomfort before placing ourselves in her hands. For us new boys it seemed like a long way from home.

Our days were controlled by bells starting at 7 am. Wash, dress, and another bell for us to assemble in the playground for our morning 'walk' whatever the weather.

This was more like a route march with the Headmaster striding out in the lead.

The older boys immediately behind him, strode out much like Olympic road walkers to keep up, whilst the new boys were at the rear having to run to maintain contact.

The direction would vary from day to day; the Memorial Park across the Kenilworth Road, the wooded and undulating common land alongside the Kenilworth Road or towards the city and around the municipal gardens. It must have appeared a regular very strange and amusing sight to onlookers and passing traffic.

There was a bell for breakfast and then again for mid-morning 1/3 pint bottle of milk time, lunch, tea, the start and end of each class, evening playtime, homework period, to dormitory and lights out time.

We had been warned by Miss Gray on our arrival that what was put on our plates was to be eaten. There were no exceptions.

There were a number of food items I loathed, like rice pudding, tapioca, and 'bread and dripping' but which I could manfully stomach. However excessive amounts of fat were insurmountable.

Fortunately I discovered a satisfactory solution. The problem could be carefully disposed of onto the wooden parquet flooring beneath the dining table and with careful footwork, massaged in. No-one ever noticed or questioned the excessive shine on the wood flooring in this area.

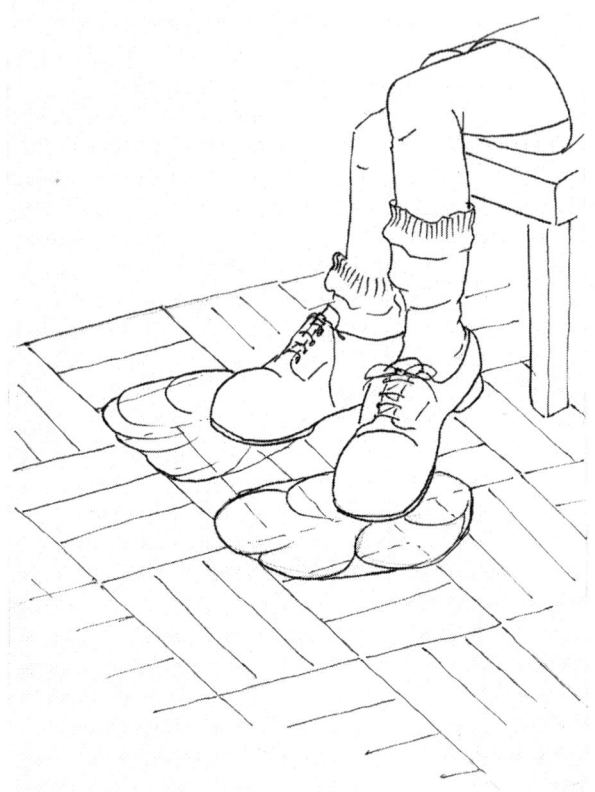

After lunch we were issued with our daily ration of two sweets, years later increased to three.

There were two other ways of increasing your sweet consumption, one legal and the second a capital offence.

As a reward for good work or some outstanding performance you could be issued with a sweet cheque payable to whomever for the value of 'so many'.

The day boys who made up the large majority of the school could bring in what sweets they liked but selling them to boarders was a severe crime for which the purchasers would be caned by the Head. Brother Peter was an unfortunate recipient on one occasion.

There would be a homework period each evening following tea and then playtime.

Each of us was permitted a small suitcase which had to contain any toys etc we wished to keep at school and also our writing pad to write the compulsory letter home every Wednesday.

A great variety of sports were encouraged, football, cricket, athletics, tennis, soft ball, airgun shooting (senior boys only), swimming in the unheated outside pool, PT squads and deck tennis.

And of course all the usual playground games, fag cards, marbles, conkers, bean bag (a form of touch rugby), cops and robbers and, in the freezing periods, ice slides.

Friday afternoon and Father arrived in the Talbot to drive us back through the centre of Coventry.

Every fourth week we would stop for a haircut in Hertford Street followed by a visit to the Geisha Cafe immediately across the road for a pineapple juice and cake; the waitresses were so smartly dressed in their black and white outfits.

Then a regular stop off at the junk shop on Far Gosford Street to spend our one shilling pocket money. Toy soldiers and Indians to add to my collection, also stink bombs in their small glass files (I still have two; I know ... so, so sad!)

Sixty odd years later and Joe and Daisy, our grandchildren are getting as much enjoyment out of the lead and plastic figures as I ever did.

And then we had a whole weekend back on the farm to find that the world for us had not irrevocably changed after all.

Historical Note

The first post war Coventry Godiva Pageant was in 1951 for the Festival of Britain. It was a huge procession; 60 tableaux illustrating historical and industrial aspects of the city. The organiser obtained 1500 period costumes and some real elephants to represent the elephant and castle arms of the city of Coventry. It was a 5-mile long procession with Lady Godiva on her horse surrounded by lines of nuns.

The procession travelled along Kenilworth Road and the Headmaster had arranged for scaffolding and raised seating to be constructed on the sports field bordering the road so that all the boys would have a perfect view. It was a spectacle that would remain with many of the boys who witnessed it.

The Godiva aspect since then has been largely lost and been replaced by the Coventry Carnival.

The Reverend Kenelm Swallow died in 1979 and on his death his medals, including his Military Cross and many personal archives were discovered in the attic of the old school building. The Military Cross was awarded to him in 1918 for returning to 'no man's land' five times to rescue wounded men.

I hadn't had cause to revisit Coventry for perhaps fifty years but when I did in 2014 I walked to the old school. Whilst it did retain some of its original buildings especially the main house where we boarders ate and slept, of course much had changed.

The school was no longer CPS but now part of King Henry VIII School with many new classes and the perimeter surrounded by wrought iron railings with locked gates.

I spoke to one of the non-teaching staff through the fence. He had recently had to dispose of all the old team photographs that I remembered hanging in the gallery. He said if I'd appeared only three weeks earlier I could have had my pick of them. As it was he went off and returned with the original copies of the CPS magazine for me from 1953 to 1957. Re-reading them reminded me of my old school friends.

The Bees

Following the death of my father a few years ago, I was clearing his house when I discovered two sealed boxes stored in the spacious cupboard under the stairs.

On opening them and removing a copy of the Daily Telegraph dated 1987 that lay on top, I discovered, not quite pots of gold, but something close.

Honey ... seventy-two jars of it!

Father had kept bees from the early 1950's and, depending on the number of swarms, the number of hives varied but there were usually half-a-dozen.

The cache looked, smelt and tasted good, though possibly a little darker than it once was. I was assured by expert apiarists at our local Swallowfield Show that as honey had survived from the pyramids, 25 or 30 years was much like yesterday.

We will be enjoying it for quite some time.

The Telegraph edition matched the year father had retired and sold the farm. I had spent many happy hours watching him with his smoker and head net opening and extracting the combs from the hives; then helping with the spinning out of the honey after he'd sliced off the wax covering.

As a lad I would spend long periods watching the bees on hot summer days returning to their hives overloaded with pollen and nectar presumably relieved to collapse onto their landing board.

Occasionally there were frantic 'dog-fights' when small numbers of wasps rashly attempted a raid on the beehives. The fights were desperate.

The wasps were able to use their stings multiple times but they were hopelessly outnumbered.

With each bee able to use its sting but once, many died as a result. So obsessed and single minded were the defenders that they continued to attack the dead attackers, thoughtless of their own survival.

Whenever anyone referred to the bees, in those days, it often led to some confusion as another species performed at Brandon Speedway stadium about five miles away.

The glow of the floodlights was easily visible across our fields.

The Brandon Bees had considerable support back in the late 1940's and 50's, the gates often exceeding 20,000, and our father and his bachelor brother who lived next door at White Stacks were two of their regulars.

When Pete and I reached six years of age we were considered old enough to join them but there were certain strings attached. It was deemed absolutely essential that we had a two hour sleep in the sitting room each speedway afternoon.

This was a complete waste of time.

We never managed to get to sleep however hard we tried. It was difficult to occupy the time as Nan would enter unexpectedly and it was wise for us to appear asleep when this occurred.

I think, even now, I could reproduce the complex pattern on the sofa material as there was little else to occupy the time.

With two friends, two trikes, a bicycle and a scooter, Pete and I re-created our own speedway races in the farmyard, even devising our own elastic starting tape.

But we couldn't wait for the real thing.

Father and Uncle John would stand on the tiered concrete steps at their favourite position alongside the track. During each race we boys would be perched on their shoulders for a perfect view. The grit flew, the racing was close and the pile-ups frequent.

We were allowed to wander off between races to explore but had to memorise the numbered floodlight nearest our position and we had to return to our high seats for the start of each race.

There wasn't a moment of inaction - the smell of the fuel, the appearance between each race of the track staff in their yellow and black striped tops and black berets who always strode on smartly armed with their rakes on their shoulders to a background military march, the Ferguson tractor with its metal rack-harrow circling the track to re-level the surface. The Woody Woodpecker song and 'cigarettes and whisky and wild, wild women, they drive you crazy they drive you insane' music blared out over the loudspeakers between races, and then the noise and the spills of the races themselves meant never ending excitement. Johnnie Reason was my hero.

Even the names of the opposition were exciting; Oxford Cheetahs, Motherwell Eagles, Walthamstow Wolves Leicester Hunters, Ashfield Giants, Chadley Heath Heathens and Glasgow White City Tigers; all sporting their team emblem on their colourful leather riding jerkins.

I recall Coventry Bees racing against Glasgow Tigers one Saturday and by coincidence Uncle Derek visited us the following week. I don't think Uncle Derek was a proper Uncle but he was a friend of Fathers'.

On his infrequent visits he would regale us with tales of his visits to India. He must have been quite a celebrity over there as the Indian authorities would contact him when they had problems with man-eaters tigers.

He might visit India for several weeks each time to identify, stalk and eventually shoot these 'problem' animals and the thankful villagers would hold Sahib Derek White in high regard.

On one visit to the farm he unfurled a huge tiger skin (with its head with teeth bared and glass eyes) on our sitting room floor.

Peter and I couldn't imagine such an enormous beast and we later discussed just how many villagers it must have eaten to get to that size.

But to get back on track; following the final meeting of the season there was a magnificent firework display and this was definitely a high point of the season.

We collected the riders' autographs and became proud club members from 1950 to 1954 sporting the Coventry Speedway Bees badge and alternate yellow and black year bars.

And then to round off the evening - the grand finale - on the way home we stopped at the Walsgrave-on-Sowe Fish and Chip shop. (chips 6d and fish 1/4d or 1/8d).

We would hold on to the hot newspaper wrapped bundles in the back of the car and invariably fall asleep and need waking up to eat them when we got back to the farm.

This presumably convinced Nan that we needed even longer sleeps on speedway afternoons!

In 2007 I revisited Brandon stadium with my daughter Rachel. Between races we dropped in to the bees supporters shop to buy a 2007 year bar to add to my 1950, 51, 52, 53, 54 bars.

The ancient salesman admired my old bees badge and year bars but his £60 offer could not prise it off me.

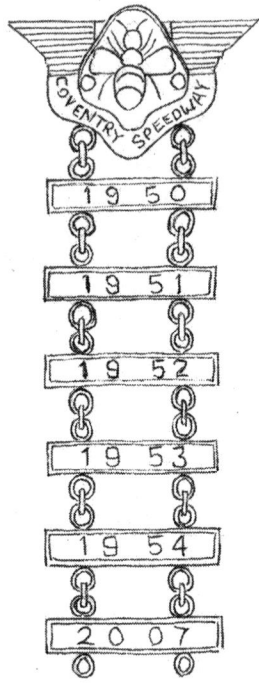

It is with sadness that I read in a recent edition of the Coventry Telegraph that speedway racing had ceased at Brandon Stadium and there were plans to build up to 250 homes on the site.

After a long running row over its future the stadium has remained derelict and many of its fixtures and fittings have been removed. Nevertheless the Club owner, Mick Horton, says he is still hoping to get the Bees back on track.

Currently, however, it is reported to be occupied by travellers.

The Ones that Got Away

Our satchel contained all that you would expect to find in a fishing bag; hooks, spare line, lead weights, floats, a disgorger, a small knife, ground-bait and a square Oxo tin housing our maggots. Pete had pierced the tin lid with several small holes to allow the maggots 'to breathe'. Considering the size of the tin and the number of maggots I tried to convince him this was probable unnecessary but Pete was always considerate about animal welfare; irrespective that they were due to be stuck on a hook, submerged and then eaten ... if we were lucky.

We had learnt to swim and had acquired a fishing rod, so were allowed to carry our gear across the fields, through the tunnel under the railway embankment, across another couple of fields to the towpath on the Oxford canal.

Nan always insisted that we had to be back for lunch or tea as she downright refused to make sandwiches to take with us; the thought of them sharing a bag with the exhaled air from our maggot tin was something she viewed with horror.

We spent many happy hours beside the canal collecting our meagre catch in a small keep-net and there seemed never any danger of us falling in, provided we avoided getting entangled with the frequently passing barges. Many of these were carrying coal to Oxford from the Warwickshire coalfields.

When it was time to return to the farm we would count our catch and release them back into the canal.

On other occasions we would visit our cousins' farm and join John and Alastair fishing in one of their sizeable ponds. Our catch was mostly roach though on rare occasions a much larger golden carp - fortunately for it, inedible.

Today, however, was to be different. Father was taking us in the car over towards Lutterworth. He had bought us a couple of nets and had negotiated with the kind lady who ran the village shop the loan of eight very large glass sweet jars (empty!) with screw lids.

It was evidently a fishing trip but other than having to wear our wellington boots we were left in the dark about just what this entailed.

We arrived at our planned destination to find a long queue of heavy lorries, loaded with soil and rubble, presumably waiting for a signal to proceed.

But proceed with just what?

A fishing trip that involved lorry loads of subsoil and aggregate was something not covered in 'Angler's Weekly'.

We impatiently awaited further developments.

Nearby was a small river that meandered along and over time had left an ox-bow completely cut off from the more direct new channel. This cut-off piece of water appeared much like a long curved pond and evidently it was to be filled to allow a road widening or building project.

The lorries started tipping their loads into the water progressively from one end. We were to stand well clear until eventually, perhaps a couple of hours later, the filling-in was virtually complete.

The volume of water had by this time been considerably reduced and we could see the accumulation of fish that were being concentrated in their fast disappearing environment.

The drivers of the last two or three lorries delayed off-loading whilst we and several other fellow 'anglers' waded into the shallow waters and scooped up the fish into whatever containers we had all managed to acquire; in our case the sweet jars. It took us no time at all to fill our containers.

We loaded up the car and started home. We returned to the lane that crossed over our canal and introduced the rescued fish into the waters there; their new home.

We wondered however just why father had kept back about a dozen of them... until he drove back to the farm and pulled into the gateway of the Slang.

The Slang was an unusual field, long and narrow and 'landed' long ago to aid drainage.

On its bottom side it had natural springs which never dried up even in long periods of drought and father had fed a couple of these springs into large concrete troughs as a watering facility for the grazing cattle.

He introduced the last of our catch; six into each trough.

Over the following twelve or so years before I left the farm for Agricultural College, whenever I wandered across the Slang I would investigate these water troughs and never failed to find some of the off-spring of the original 'ones that had got away'.

Now perhaps sixty-five years after our rescue mission, I can still see the concrete water troughs in the Slang as I drive along the lane from Withybrook towards Shilton.

But I doubt I'll ever take a closer look.

Pulling Power

Ever since we boys were very small, father had made a special effort in preparing for the annual bonfire event or so it seemed to us. But to a large degree it was just a part of running the farm.

In the years following the war, the fields tended to be relatively small and the hedges and ditches took up a disproportionate area of potentially productive land.

So over the years when labour was not required elsewhere the Fordson Major tractor (1948 model) and heavy chain were employed in the strenuous task of extracting some of these hedges leaving the additional jobs of piping in the ditches and levelling the ground.

This in itself had considerable entertainment value.

The heavy chain which encircled the roots was attached to the hook on the underside of the tractor which then accelerated away from a standing start until it had taken up the slack.

The front wheels of the tractor would rear into the air as the tractor's forward motion was suddenly halted. But with repeated efforts the stubborn roots would eventually surrender their hold.

This resulted in a tremendous quantity of 'fuel' which over the weeks was assembled into a giant heap in front of the spinney.

There were plenty of retained hedges of course which themselves would periodically require cutting or cutting and laying to maintain them in good condition and the cuttings would be added to the pile.

The Fordson Major had to put up with some pretty rough treatment and even the chain would break on rare occasions

All farm implements seemed, in time, to develop their own idiosyncrasies and our Fordson Major was no exception.

I recall that a heavy gate hook had to be attached to the accelerator cable or rather the governor in order to control the engine revs.

The sudden deceleration when the chain slack was taken up and the resulting rearing up of the front of the tractor sometimes dislodged this vital piece of equipment.

This caused some consternation for the tractor driver and anyone else standing in the near vicinity as the engine revs would increase to a terrifying rate until the gate hook could be located and repositioned.

The dislodged hook on occasions was difficult to find in the undergrowth and there was a distinct possibility the engine block and pistons would explode.

At times when there had been some delay in finding the detached accessory it was a difficult decision to know whether to race back towards the tractor with it or retire in some haste to a safe distance.

Provided it retained its gate hook and you didn't break your thumb on the starting handle the Major was a sturdy and reliable work horse.

The heap of roots and branches grew as did our anticipation as November approached.

The position of the fire was important. It needed to be between the spinney and Gran's house so she could see it from her sitting room.

The 'Guy' who was always fitted with a pair of worn out wellingtons, was positioned on top with the aid of a long ladder and a four wheeled trailer was drawn up to windward of the bonfire.

Many of our classmates from the village school would be invited and would arrive bearing a donation of fireworks which father would store in a box beneath the trailer.

These would be extracted, as required to be placed in sand-trays on the trailer so everyone could get a good view, including Gran.

Father never failed to get the giant heap ignited even in the wettest of conditions, occasionally having to resort

to several bales of straw and the potentially dangerous addition of petrol.

In the early years we wrapped potatoes in silver foil and placed them in the fire but this exercise generally proved a failure.

Mrs Beeton's recommended timing for a super-crispy skin was 1½ to 2 hours at 180°F; unfortunately temperature control was impossible and duration only of any significance if you could remember where you'd put them in the first place.

Often they were only discovered in the ashes the following day – the silver wrappings still in their ball shape but the contents completely incinerated.

The entertainment value of the bonfire would extend well into the following week. This included the challenge to find the rocket sticks in the surrounding countryside and to keep the tree stumps and hedge roots burning, perhaps for an additional 4 or 5 days.

A most unlikely event was to occur on this precise bonfire spot 50 or so years later.

Of course in the intervening period many things had changed – the farm had been sold and the land absorbed by surrounding farms.

Father had moved out of the farmhouse into a new house he had had built in the old farm garden. This enabled him in retirement to still look out onto his old fields and the spinney.

One afternoon father received a noisy and rather disjointed telephone call from our son, David, requesting him to sit himself comfortably on his garden seat on the raised front lawn.

He thought this a most unusual request but he did as he had been asked, intrigued about what might be in store.

The giant twin-rotor Chinook helicopter made two tight and noisy circuits overhead checking for animals then descended to bonfire height in front of the spinney barely 100yards away, hovered, flashed its lights and bowed twice before peeling away.

David's flight had taken him directly over the house and whilst it had not involved him making any deviation to his flight plan, he had given his Grandfather a thrill he would always remember.

In truth he'd nearly blown him away!

Miss Perry
and her English Exercises

Before I arrived in the fifth form at Coventry Preparatory School I was aware of Miss Perry.

She was a slim, attractive (though my judgement might have been suspect at that tender age), reasonably tall lady and seemed to have a well-stocked wardrobe of smart clothes. These included brightly coloured high-heeled shoes, body-hugging skirts and low cut blouses.

Miss Perry lived in a house on a neighbouring estate within half a mile of the school, so within easy walking distance.

I say 'easy', but in her high heels and a tight skirt it would have been anything but.

Possibly she changed from more comfortable walking shoes into her raised heels only when she approached the school premises though I couldn't imagine her employing a similar strategy with her skirt.

She would invariably be wearing a long coat to maintain her modesty until she entered her classroom.

She would then hang her coat on the hook behind the door and appear seemingly all ready for the cat-walk.

We 10 year old boys had never been exposed to such an apparition and Miss Perry was to teach us English when we reached the lofty heights of the 5th and 6th forms as eleven and twelve year olds.

Even in hindsight I find it difficult to credit that she could appear at school each day in such attire.

I can only assume that she was extremely well qualified which was the primary concern of the Headmaster, the Reverend Kenelm Swallow; and none of her fellow teachers (all male in the Upper School) would be likely to raise any objection.

Our English lessons followed a set procedure. Phase 1 and Miss Perry would be seated on her high stool facing us from behind her desk with the blackboard a few restricted strides away.

Whenever she rose to write on the blackboard the tightness of her skirt became apparent. Could she really be comfortable wearing such constraining clothes?

She would then return to her stool.

After about half-an-hour or so of this routine she would straighten her back and we boys knew we were due to enter phase 2 and we were about to plunge into a time-warp and be transported to a strange new world.

I should mention at this stage that Miss Perry had a well-endowed bookshelf that was evident but not excessively so, above her rather risqué blouse.

After straightening her back she would stand, push back her high stool, stretch and place her hands in close proximity to each other on the desk-top in front of her.

Keeping her arms straight ... she would then lean ever so slowly forward.

Now, even those readers without an engineering degree can foresee what was about to occur.

As she leaned even further forward so her forearms, acting much like bookends to her book-shelf, forced her two volumes inwards and upwards.

She would remain in this position for perhaps two or three minutes though none of us would be looking at the clock.

She could have been speaking in a foreign tongue and no one in her class would have noticed. We were completely mesmerised and holding our collective breath.

Would her two volumes topple off; they did seem precariously balanced?

Then she would lean back and re-station herself on her stool.

Gravity re-asserted itself and everything subsided, settling into their allotted place and we boys would come back down to Earth and inhale normally once more.

None of us spoke to each other about what we regularly witnessed; it almost felt like a collective secret.

We might not have had a thorough grasp of her perfect participles or conjunctive adverbs but I defy any of her past pupils to deny they remember their Miss Perry with anything but a lasting fondness.

On the Fiddle

Father had evidently been waiting all week for a still, windless day. This was a requirement for such jobs as spraying when even a slight breeze would cause drift.

I was on holiday from school, but spraying was not the operation he had in mind for me today.

He had 6 acres all prepared ready for sowing grass seed and this was to be applied using a fiddle. The fiddle was a pretty ancient implement that I'd seen used only once before; it was a hand operated tool that took its name from the fiddle like action required to broadcast the seeds.

The device was suspended by a shoulder strap and consisted of a canvas seed bag and wooden hopper with a horizontal mounted finned disc beneath, which was rotated in alternating directions by means of a hand operated leather-thonged bow.

The leather chord that ran the length of the wooden bow took a turn round the finned disk spindle so that on each stroke of the bow the disk would spin first clockwise and then on the reverse stroke, anti-clockwise.

As the 3 foot long bow was moved from one side to the other, with each forward step, so the regulated flow of seed landing on the disc would be flung out in a semi-circle. The range depended on the type of seed.

Six acres sounded like I was in for a long walk, but Father was planning his own up-to-date development. He was going to partially mechanise the system by sitting me facing forward on the front of the tractor bonnet.

He would drive and I would fiddle away whilst gripping onto the sides of the tractor with my legs.

Father had been brought up to make do and mend and very little was ever thrown away. Tools and implements, if they had something to commend them, were never discarded solely on account of their age and he evidently thought the fiddle, which seemed to me to have survived from biblical times, still had some merit.

As you might surmise, the front end of the tractor was not the most secure of positions; there was very little traction between me and the bonnet and even a slight touch of the tractor brakes would have me sliding off the front; but I had every confidence Dad would notice my absence in time to avoid running me over.

I think it's fair to say I wouldn't have had quite so much confidence if my twin brother Peter had been behind the wheel, remembering just what a hard time he gave me on the trailer when we were carting bales!

This was my first experience of using this ancient contraption and I was aware that it was important to maintain a steady forward speed and consistent fiddling action otherwise the seed would not be evenly spread.

Leaving an area unsown would be embarrassingly evident when the seed germinated.

It was an interesting phenomenon that farmers were always more careful when drilling or ploughing roadside fields as a blocked seed drill or dog-legged furrow was evident to passing neighbours and a source for general discussion and debate in the local pub.

I always made an extra effort under such circumstances.

I hadn't ever witnessed anyone fiddling whilst riding on the tractor bonnet before but I wasn't about to question it or complain as it was going to save me a long trek.

So Dad maintained a steady speed and kept the correct distance from his previous wheel marks.

I just had to keep up an even fiddling action and sing out to him when my seed hopper was running low, requiring a refill.

We completed the novel operation without mishap.

When we'd finished the sowing, I linked up to the chain harrows to run over the field again to cover the seeds and then rolled it with the flat roller to complete the process.

Ideally it would have saved an operation if we could have trailed the harrows behind the tractor whilst sowing but this would have covered the wheel marks which Dad needed as a guide on the next run across.

Whilst this development that Dad had devised had proved pretty successful, the tractor bonnet was not the most comfortable of sitting positions.

If this was to become a regular job for me, a cushion and securing rope or even a saddle with stirrups (if we still had one from pony days) might be an improvement!

Velcro, if it had been invented, would have been a solution. It is certainly now used in Middle-East camel racing to prevent their young jockeys becoming detached.

This semi-mechanised fiddling technique would not be possible today as roll bars and tractor cabs are now compulsory and the regulations emphasise that you must be *inside* them!

Finer Points

Every year a recognised judge of Ayrshire cows appeared on the farm to assess both the dairy herd and their young-stock replacements.

It was an annual competition open to all Ayrshire herds in Warwickshire and over the years father had had more than his share of success.

However, he had never taken individual animals to local agricultural shows and this year he'd decided to do so.

This was not something that could be achieved on the spur of the moment. It required a degree of planning and preparation.

There are many different show classes, but father was aiming to enter animals in the in-milk heifer (having had her first calf) and in-milk junior cow (having had her second calf) classes. Perhaps it should be mentioned here that animals would be shown perhaps 5 to 10 weeks after calving to look at their best.

So it had to be decided which shows to aim for and their dates, which animals in the herd could be possible contenders, would they be likely to calve at the right time and could they be relied upon to behave themselves away from home?

The possible candidates then had to be trained.

Up to this time all the animals that had had their first calf would already be accustomed to a neck tie when in the cowshed but being led on a halter was a different matter. This was often an exercise fraught with difficulty.

I imagine breaking in a horse would be more involved but that didn't mean cows or particularly young heifers were without problems.

The farmyard, surrounded by farm buildings on all sides, was the best option. When any of them decided to use their weight advantage to make a break for freedom they could only go so far.

But with perseverance and leading them out each day they got accustomed to the idea.

Then it was a matter of getting them to walk at a sedate pace, stop and stand in the best position or stance, get used to being handled and to some degree get used to the odd noises or sights that they might experience at a showground.

As the event approached some of the cow's coat would be clipped out, around the shoulders, along its back and a little on its belly to make the underline continue in a straight line with the udder, then thorough scrubbing with soap and water.

There was quite a bit of tinkering that could be done to make an animal look its best.

Some would use chalk powder on the udder or even a form of adhesive on the inner side of the teats to make an ideal shape (frowned on by most competitors) and marked down when detected by a judge.

The Warwickshire County Ayrshire Club also had a herdsmen's judging competition. This gave all herdsmen in the county an opportunity to test their skills (or luck) in judging the finer points of animal conformation.

During the course of the year different herds in the Midlands would host an open evening on their farms; this would involve a farm walk and a look around their herd followed by refreshments.

The host farmer was also requested to select and parade 6 of his cows for the herdsmen and a guest master judge to place in order of merit.

During the course of the year perhaps 6 of these events took place and were assessed for an overall winner.

Several of the judges had shown their animals at major shows and they each would have slightly different views on just what constituted the ideal specimen.

So to some extent it was selecting the order you thought the judge would make rather than perhaps your own preference.

The club would also hold an annual dinner, often at a hotel but occasionally on a member's farm.

This year father had volunteered.

As our herd was primarily autumn calving this meant that almost all had been 'dried off' by late summer. They were enjoying life out in the fields awaiting their next calf without the distraction or interruption of being milked twice each day.

This left the cowshed empty and for a couple of weeks before the annual dinner it was thoroughly scrubbed, de-cobwebbed, and re-snowcemed until it shone like new.

It was decorated with sheaves of corn around the pillars, flowers and plenty of straw bales as casual seating. A double row of trestle tables ran the length of the shed along with seating and in the corner was a well-stocked straw-baled bar.

It looked a picture and I wondered whether going into countryside catering might be more financially rewarding than milking!

Large mobile cooking vehicles arrived in the yard early on the day to provide the main course and a vast selection of cheeses and fruit comprised dessert.

About 70-80 attended and it was quite a spectacular evening.

There followed the regulation speeches and awards and to my surprise I was awarded the herdsmen's judging tankard!

This was to be a mixed blessing as along with the award was the dubious honour of being 'elected' assistant judge at the Grand Annual Autumn Show and Sale held at Reading Cattle Market. This was a major event in the dairy cattle world in those days.

I surmised that this would entail a long drive, fetching and carrying for the master judge, handing out rosettes, running errands and fetching coffee.

I would also need to negotiate with the Principal of Shuttleworth Agricultural College for a Monday off in order for me to take up my new position; as I was leaving Warwickshire for Bedfordshire in a couple of weeks.

The Ten Bob Note

Mike Ings was a little eccentric.

As I've mentioned previously, our fathers were neighbouring farmers back home in Warwickshire and Mike rode their hunting horses at Point to Points.

I'd spent some convivial winter evenings with him sitting in front of an open fire when his parents were out, drinking his father's whisky whilst Paddy, his sister, kindly rustled up hot buttered toast.

It was early October 1963 and Mike and I had arrived at Shuttleworth Agricultural College.

Mike, I recall, was well endowed with suits and on our arrival I entered into discussions to purchase one of them. After lengthy and unsuccessful negotiations, with me trying to beat him down from £1 10/- to a pound, I eventually gave in and agreed to his inflated price.

However I had to concede it did fit me remarkably well and, I finished up pleased with my purchase.

After checking through the pockets I was surprised to discover a pristine, orange 10/- note (ten shillings in old money) in the inside pocket.

Was this left there by mistake, was it 'good luck money' or did Mike feel guilty at overcharging me? I somehow doubted that.

To my discredit I failed to pursue the matter with him and as it was such an excellent un-creased specimen I added it to my numismatic collection.

I will return to this ten shillings later.

Mike had a blue Riley 1.6 and on the occasions he wished to drive at speed he would don a crash helmet which he kept at other times on his back seat. I guess this was an attempt at self-preservation from his horse riding days.

Perhaps it should be mentioned here that these were days before safety belts and drink driving regulations.

We were barely into our third week of term when he failed to negotiate the Biggleswade A1 roundabout. This was a rather unforgiving obstacle, more like a small hillock and he had no option but to leave his car marooned there.

He completed the appropriate accident forms and despatched them to his insurance company.

It was with some widespread incredulity that no sooner had he been reunited with his repaired vehicle than he repeated the accident on the very same island.

Surely this was an accomplishment that had not been achieved before or since.

The now familiar insurance forms arrived and where it requested a drawing to illustrate the accident, he wrote,

'Ditto (see previous accident).'

There had been a worrying number of car accidents during that first term and Ken Russell, our principal, gave the assembled year a severe lecturing and a serious warning that such dangerous behaviour must cease.

The following weekend I'd driven three college friends in my mini-van (with a fold-up rear seat) into Bedford to attend a dance laid on by the Bedford Teacher Training College.

Shuttleworth had a good symbiotic affiliation with both the Bedford PE College and the Teachers Training College whereby we supported their functions and they ours.

This association led to many long term relationships including my own.

Our college was extremely fortunate to have 3 very talented musicians and a lead singer who had formed themselves into a 'group'.

They were aptly named 'Virus Yellows and the Sugar Beets' and they had a slot that evening. Many fellow students felt certain that if they stayed together, had a good manager and abandoned any idea of a future in agriculture, a successful career in the pop industry was assured.

It was a great night … with the exception that we left the road at Cardington on our return trip and finished in a deep ditch.

Fortunately there were no serious injuries.

Inevitably I was ordered to see the Principal in his office. After his severe warning issued barely a week before, I feared the worst. Could my time at college be prematurely terminated? This seemed a distinct possibility.

There was a long silence as he tapped his fingers on his desktop seemingly in deep meditation.

'What are we going to do with you?' This was followed by another long silence.

He opened the large diary on his desk and slowly turned the pages. Was he deciding just when I should leave?

'I see here that you are due to go to the Reading Cattle Market next Monday to be the assistant judge at their annual show and sale. Well, with your vehicle off the road you won't be able to go.' He proceeded to draw a line through the entry in his diary, looked at me and said 'Let that be a lesson to you, my boy.'

Looking suitably chastened I left his study feeling greatly relieved to have escaped so very lightly and if truth be known I felt missing out on the Reading trip was no great loss.

Historical note:

2013 and I had been given the responsibility of rounding up as many of the 1963/65 course members I could and persuade them to attend a reunion at Shuttleworth, in our case '50 year' although it was a weekend open to all old students.

I was delighted that Mike Ings was to attend and following the Saturday night dinner I reminded him of his suit sale fifty years previously, asking if he'd intentionally left a 10/- note in the pocket.

'No way Rob, you must be joking!'' he exclaimed.

I extracted the very same note from my pocket and returned it to him.

I believe he still thinks this was a joke that I'd concocted … but, it was the truth.

The Kenilworth Incident

Hello. This looks like trouble!

We had been showing three of our Ayrshires at the Kenilworth Agricultural Show and all had gone as well as we could have hoped.

We'd been awarded a first and third for the two freshly calved heifers and a second for the 'second - calver', in their respective classes.

Our three animals were tethered in the cattle lines awaiting the call from the stewards to join the Grand Parade, the final cattle event in the main show-ring. This involved all the livestock being led in procession around the periphery and drawn up in their breed groups abreast of one another in the centre of the ring.

Father, Fred (our herdsman) and I were about to untie the halters of our three from their berths in the cattle lines when there appeared to be a sudden disturbance amongst a group of spectators.

A Shorthorn bull, being led around the ground by the farmer and his wife team, had evidently been spooked.

Mrs, who had been holding the strong wooden pole (bull staff), which was attached to the bull's nose-ring, and the main means of controlling the animal, had been jerked off her feet.

But she was valiantly endeavouring to hang on whilst being dragged along the turf.

Mr, who had hold of the rope halter on the other side of the animal could not control the near 1 ton beast as it decided to get its head beneath the ring-side rope and force its way through the panicking spectators.

They, up to that point had been sitting on straw bales and wooden benches, eating sandwiches and ice-creams and watching the sedate procession go by.

Mrs had no chance of regaining her feet and had been forced to release the pole as she was buffeted by the passing straw bales and abandoned picnic baskets.

Mr was now on his own, on his feet and travelling at some speed - still with a hold on the rope halter but with no pretence of being in control.

The bull had decided to career along the cattle lines towards us.

They passed by in something of a blur followed by Mrs in her green-stained white coat who was attempting to regain contact.

How and where was the rodeo going to end? Perhaps some brave soul might grab hold of the flailing bull staff or the rampaging animal could eventually tire; hopefully before he reached the showground carpark or even the china shop in the nearby town!

There was a mains water stand-pipe positioned at the end of each of the cattle lines and with some considerable presence of mind under the fraught circumstances Mr took a couple of swift turns of the rope halter around the pipe just below the tap as they sped by ...

and hung on.

Of course the momentum was bound to cause some collateral damage.

The water facility had not been designed with such treatment in mind.

Would the galvanised piping shear off and add to the debris trailing along behind the runaways?

By some miracle it held, although the vertical pipe was now straightened out at ground level with the farmer on his knees but still grimly holding on.

As if the situation needed an extra twist of fate, inevitably the pipe fractured and a fountain of water (at 40 psi) was drenching both Mr and the bull.

Mrs, red-faced and perspiring copiously from either over exertion or extreme embarrassment, arrived in time to grasp the pole and the chaotic situation was once more coming under control.

We quickly joined the parade with our three animals and with the exception of the geyser and a steward desperately looking for a stopcock, all was getting back to normal.

Whilst the scattered spectators repositioned the straw bales, righted the wooden benches, got re-acquainted with their partly consumed picnics and resettled themselves, the bedraggled trio returned to their cattle wagon.

They'd had their early bath – it was time to go home.

Farm Sale

**Shilton Farm
(5 miles Coventry & Nuneaton)**

Hackney & Sons

Are instructed by Mr J. P. Grindal to offer for sale by Auction on

<u>Friday, April 3rd, 1987</u>

<u>72 Cattle</u>

<u>Implements, Machinery etc</u>

<u>20 ton approx. Baled Hay</u>

<u>Sale to commence at 11.30 am prompt</u>

Light Refreshments Available

This would be a sad day.

Father had worked on the farm his whole life and that life had not been easy.

His father had died in a loft fall when he was only three and his mother was left to raise the 4 children. Uncle Kitt, a relative and a hard taskmaster had run the farm until father was old enough to take over. Father then lost his wife (my mother) when my twin brother and I were born.

He gave us boys a 'fun' upbringing, a good schooling, bred arguably one of the finest dairy herds of Ayrshires in the Midlands and been elected by his fellow dairy farmers to represent them as one of 12 national members on the Milk Marketing Board for twelve consecutive years.

But since the 1970's and 1980's the writing had been on the wall. The British mixed farm that was a creation of the enclosures of the 18th and 19th centuries was fast disappearing. Its purpose was to combine livestock and arable so that if one part of the business failed there were always others acting as a back-up. Additionally there was an interlinking of production in that you could feed the crops you'd grown to the animals and fertilize the land with the animal manure.

This all seems eminently sensible.

But now scale of production, consistency of product and efficiency were the requirements to supply the processing plants and the supermarkets that were replacing the local grocer and butcher etc.

In many respects the change this has wrought on the farming community and village life has been detrimental. In Shilton there's now one pub instead of two, the local shop and newsagent have disappeared and the post office closed. Although the railway line still passes though the village, the station has gone, as has the tank engine shunting goods wagons into the sidings.

So farming had progressed and 130 acres and 35 milking cows plus their followers, once seen to be a reasonable size herd was no longer viable and the farm was to be sold.

I took a few days off from my research work at the National Institute for Research in Dairying at Reading to help father set up for the day of the sale.

This involved constructing a sale-ring in the rick-yard and arranging for the smooth flow of cattle through the ring.

The farm tractors, machinery , implements and other farm equipment had to be arranged in individual 'lots' out in the Home Field and car parking organised for visitors on the day.

232 'lots' in all.

3 Tractors, disc mower, elevator, hedge trimmer, crop sprayer, chain harrows, Cambridge roller, dairy equipment etc.

The blacksmiths anvil, two blow lamps, quantities of ropes and cattle halters, pitch forks and yard brushes, old milk churns, a pile of hessian and large railway sacks, sack weighing platform scales etc.

And here lay a group of galvanised chicken feeders and water troughs right next to a group of hedge laying tools; two billhooks, a thick leather glove and some hedge slashers and a sharpening stone.

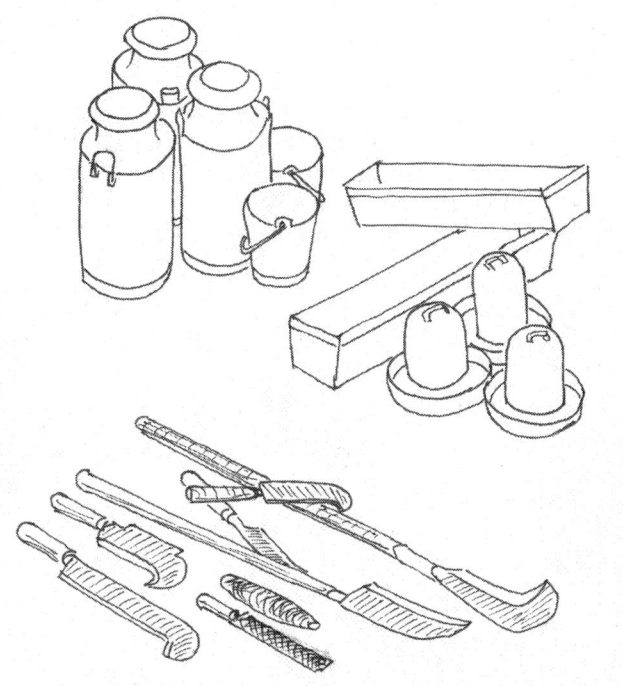

This combination of lots reminded me of my early 'pigs ear' attempts at hedge laying. Father had stood there watching for a while before commenting 'You look like an old hen scratching for daylight'.

It wasn't said maliciously but any job not meeting his standard of acceptability and you'd expect this or the shortened version 'looks like you're scratching for daylight'.

They all looked so out of place in their small groups out in the field.

For so many years they had made the farm a working, viable and cohesive living entity; each of the now sad looking and isolated items playing their important and critical role in a functioning agricultural enterprise.

It only needed a comment or innocuous remark to bring back so many memories and seemingly long forgotten events.

I looked across to the Dutch barn and there was Pete and I climbing from a stack of straw bales onto the barn's corrugated tin roof to slide down the other side to lodge our heels in the rusting gutter with old Mr Bolton in his garden two doors away almost too afraid to move to telephone the farm to get us down.

My mind wandered across the fields to playing war-games amongst the stooked sheaves, lobbing clumps of stubble at each other over our defensive positions; and sitting, soaking up the sun by the hedge in the Big Field cradling the 12-bore when a hare ambled through the rails to sit on its haunches just a couple of yards away, one ear up and one down looking at me quizzically. We looked at each other without moving for perhaps thirty seconds before it leisurely lolloped off (and, no, I didn't shoot it!).

Father saw me standing looking wistfully at the isolated and friendless items. 'Take any bits and pieces that you want Rob' he said kindly.

Much to my wife's eternal despair I still have a quantity of hay-knives, a favourite pitch-fork, a cast iron seat off an old binder, a full roll of John Bull binder-twine, a five gallon drum of dark creosote, some numbered cattle feed buckets (with clear memories of the cows they belonged to), milk churns, old square petrol cans with brass screw caps, a pick axe, a sledge hammer and mobile forge.

And Jill will tell me there's more!

As I took a last look at the two and four wheeled trailers, there was I, stacking the hay and straw bales, sheaves and sacks of corn each harvest time.

On occasions when the nights were hot and the dews held off so that the grain stayed dry we could continue combining and hauling the sacks of grain till well after midnight. And if it was near full moon you could see so clearly what you were doing without headlights. These were some of my favourite times.

And whenever we picked up the very last sheaf, bale or sack, Dad would never fail to remark 'that's the one we've been looking for Rob!'

The day of the sale was overcast but thankfully dry.

A good crowd of 'hopefully' potential customers had turned up including many farming friends to show their support, and the sale got under-way.

There was an old 'young farmer' from my Pailton Young Farmers' Club days. Father would lend me the Morris Oxford to pick up three others on the way to the weekly meetings, Ben Parker, his brother John and then on to collect Ted Holloway from farms in Withybrook. My very first meeting, in 1961, sticks in my mind:

Girls – Demonstration on Make-up – Miss Smith
Boys – National Institute of Agricultural Engineering (diesel)

I guess that they wouldn't get away with such sexist segregation nowadays. It would perhaps be a watered down politically correct version of 'Just what to wear in your tractor cab' or similar!

It was a good sale with many of the items selling for above expected prices; I think a measure of support and respect many people had for father.

Some milking cows and the young-stock had been sold first, followed by the 'immovable' objects in the farm buildings, the stack of baled hay and finally the machinery and odd lots in the field.

I was standing alongside father as the auctioneer approached the very last 'lot' – the 'International 440 Baler'.

As the auctioneer approached the baler and announced the last lot, I didn't look at Dad, as I knew that like me, he'd have a tear in his eye.

I was waiting and more than half expecting him to make a comment and he didn't disappoint me.

'That's the one we've been looking for, Rob.'

He said it almost too quietly for me to hear … but then, I'd been listening very carefully and expecting those very words.

I put my hand on his shoulder but couldn't trust myself to say anything.

The Byre

My body ached. I couldn't breathe. Wondering why I was looking up at the underside of the four-wheeled trailer.

I lay on my back trying to get some air and remember what had just happened; then slowly crawled out from my bewildering position.

I remembered hiding amongst the bales at the top of the Dutch barn, then hearing the call for tea. I'd approached the edge of the stack, looking down to the rick-yard, way below. Perhaps the others were already back at the farm-house. I'd slipped.

It had been a long fall as the barn was almost full, probably around 18 to 20 feet.

Somehow I'd passed through the two foot gap left between the empty trailer and the vertical stack of bales before landing heavily on a small pile of loose hay. A couple of broken bales were not unusual when off-loading trailers but passing through the gap to reach them was much less likely.

At the time, being perhaps eight or nine, I didn't analyse how lucky I'd been, though I have since. If I'd caught even a glancing blow on the trailer things would have been very different.

As everything seemed to be working I decided it best not to mention the incident to anyone as it would only lead to restricted playing areas in the future. Having free run of all the farm buildings was so much fun.

The farm buildings that surrounded the farmyard, the rick-yard, the poultry pens and the Dutch barn were a wonderful playground and the risk of losing any part of it was not worth thinking about.

The old cowshed was one of my favourites. It was probably the oldest building on the farm, pre-dating the farmhouse itself though I can't explain how this could be so.

When I was four I remember standing in the old cowshed open doorway. Father was kneeling, as if in prayer with his back towards me.

What was he doing?

I had been sent across the yard by Nan to tell him his 'elevenses' was ready.

Whatever he was doing it required some concentration and I thought it best not to disturb him. I stood in the doorway patiently waiting. He was completely unaware of my presence.

He eventually leant back to sit on his heels and placed a short stick down beside him. He looked down as if scrutinising his work.

'Oh, Hello Rob' he said as I caught his eye. He waved me forward to stand beside him.

He had filled in a hole in the concrete floor with some fresh cement and I recognised my name inscribed in it. He'd indented with his stick:

ROBERT

AND PETER

1948

Father had hand-milked 12 Shorthorn cows in here before the war but now had a vacuum line and milking machine installed. But very soon a new large cowshed was to be built across the yard to house 27 milking cows and the old shed would be used to over-winter young-stock.

With a nearly permanent covering of bedding the inscription would lie unseen and forgotten.

It was early autumn in 1969 and late evening when the peaceful existence of the old cow shed was disturbed. Father and my twin brother Peter (on leave from the Royal Navy) were to hear a loud crunch. Armed with flashlights they went out into the farmyard to investigate.

There was a dim glow radiating from the old cow shed and they entered to find what they could hardly recognise as a Mini surrounded by bricks.

The car had evidently been travelling at some speed into the village, failed to negotiate the bend, crossed the pavement, demolished the next door neighbours 7 foot high garden wall and then the rear wall of the farm building.

It was an horrendous sight.

Through some miracle one of the car's headlights was still functioning. None of the three occupants were wearing the newly introduced safety belts and were probably in their late teens.

The lad in the driving seat was already dead and the two girl passengers in the back seriously injured. Whilst Father phoned the emergency services, Peter managed to reach through the smashed window-screen to switch off the ignition, and turn off the lights and still blaring radio, thinking this might reduce the chance of fire.

Because of the severe damage to the car and the brick debris it was impossible to gain access to the rear passengers.

The brick supports to the heavy wooden roof beams and A-frames of the 250 year old building were severely weakened and there was a distinct possibility the roof would collapse adding to the already chaotic situation.

The emergency services arrived in quick time and started on the difficult task of cutting out the occupants.

I visited the farm just over a month later to find the walls repaired and the young-stock in residence in their winter quarters as if nothing untoward had happened.

It went through my mind that if the accident had occurred just a fortnight later the animals would have added to the carnage.

In the early 1970's a couple of microlite enthusiasts arrived in the farmyard to ask if they could use one of our fields for take-off and landing. This was agreed and as I was at the farm that weekend they kindly offered me a flight and with some apprehension I accepted.

Seating room on the two man microlite was inevitably at a premium with just an open space beneath. Once over the very bumpy lift-off it did allow me an ideal opportunity to take some aerial photographs of the farm and farm buildings.

In the early 1980's a celebrated local artist arrived on the farm to view the farmyard and the surrounding barns. Michael Warr spent many months over two or three years creating some wonderful paintings that would be a lasting reminder of the farm's past.

One of his favourite subjects was the roof timbers and the wooden beams including the items stored on them that may have remained there undisturbed for decades.

The farm was due to be sold in 1987.

Several of these paintings father had commissioned and others I was to see in an exhibition of Warr's work at the Fine Art Trade Guild Gallery in London in 1984.

Sadly the buildings were demolished after the farm was sold with the exception of the old cowshed and as Michael Warr was having to vacate his current studio in Shilton, father agreed to convert the shed into a replacement workplace for him.

However, no sooner had a large light-admitting window, a toilet and sink been installed than the plan fell through. Michael had to move away.

For ten more years it was a cluttered storage area, until in 1999 I was given the chance to convert it to a two-bedroom cottage to use as a base when visiting father.

When the floor was thoroughly scrubbed there was the inscription still clearly visible after all the intervening years. It was inevitable that the concrete floor had to be removed to be replaced with oak floor boards.

But I could not let the inscription be destroyed.

With some considerable skill and care the builders managed to neatly cut out the 2 foot by 3 foot rectangular section and positioned it as a step just inside the new kitchen doorway.

Our daughter Rachel enjoyed living in the cottage (now named 'The Byre') for 7 years until it was eventually sold in 2016.

This finally ended my connection with the old farm although, as my wife, Jill, constantly reminds me I still have a garden shed full of clutter rescued from the farm sale and a number of lichen covered staddlestones taking over our garden.

We also have several of Michael's splendid paintings as a lasting memory and my aerial photos.

A friend was admiring one of Michael's pictures recently; a painting of a flowering plant growing across the front of the old coal-house window.

(*a sudden burst of laughter.*)

It had been on our wall for several years and it had never struck me as even mildly amusing.

I joined him and he pointed to the artist's inscription written beneath the painting.

'Hoya plant at Shilton Farm' by Michael Warr.

But,

     ... the **L** was missing from Shilton!

Note: A number of these paintings are used as illustrations in Michael Warr's book entitled 'Painting Detail in Watercolour' including Father's favourite 'Last of the Ayrshires'.

In his book the artist writes: 'The painting of a cow and calf was prompted by the fact that a dairy farmer friend of mine was retiring. He was very proud of his Shilton Ayrshire herd which stemmed back to the early forties. Obviously it was necessary to run down the herd slowly and these two were sadly the end of the line.'

I completed my research project at the National Institute for Research in Dairying (NIRD) in Shinfield, Reading and later at the Institute for Animal Health (IAH) at Compton. I then worked for a company situated on the outskirts of Reading which produced and distributed scientific equipment.

The Farm Sale at Shilton had been a bitter day for our family but the closure of the NIRD in 1985 was to cause a tangible void in the whole village of Shinfield.

Farm building decay and demolition of the research site ensued to be followed by full residential development. And the animals disappeared.

A Village Changed

(Memories of the National Institute for Research in Dairying 1921-1985 (NIRD)

March 31st 1985 and the closure of the National Institute for Research in Dairying in Shinfield was a sadder day in hindsight than it seemed at the time.

For me it meant moving on to continue my research project at the Institute for Animal Health at Compton after 20 years at the NIRD, whilst other colleagues moved to Hurley, Reading University or even North Wyke or Aberystwyth.

The sun and snow always seemed to make their timely seasonal appearances in years gone by. But then the memory plays tricks.

However it was no illusion that the NIRD was a fine place to work and 430 staff could not fail to have an impact on the village of Shinfield.

The Institute, based at the Manor and Church Farm site since 1921 and running to over 1000 acres around the village, contributed a movement and vitality. There was constant activity from agricultural staff and machinery. Before roads became so busy, there were cattle drives through the village with outriders (herdsmen on bicycles) attempting to stop all the openings! Many, if not most of the institute staff, lived in the village utilising the facilities, social and commercial.

The Institute, initially a little over 300 acres grew over the years with the purchase of Arborfield Hall Farm, which subsequently became the home of the Bernard Weitz Centre (now the Centre of Dairy Research CEDAR) with a 400 cow herd (reckoned to be the best experimental unit for milking cows in Europe), High Copse Farm, Parrot Farm and Carters Hill Farm. With other minor additions the institute had responsibility for 1113 acres, and stocked nearly 600 cows, 500 young-stock, over 1000 pigs together with some goats and sheep.

NIRD was very highly regarded both nationally and internationally for its research in the wide field of milk production and milk utilisation.

Experiments could be planned jointly with however many of the 10 departments (scientific disciplines) were required. Cooperation within and between departments was exceptional and the facilities and services and co-operation of farm-staff was considerable.

The whole establishment was fully self-contained; all professional services were 'in house'.

Red Tape was at the minimum; a benefit not fully appreciated at the time, but appreciated later by staff moving on to other establishments.

A good social life supplemented the fine working environment; from the senior common room to inter-departmental sports competitions, many staff playing for and against village teams at cricket, soccer and tennis.

But the football pitch, tennis courts, putting green, croquet lawn and gardens, immaculately tended by the gardening staff have now disappeared, even the monumental cedar which some say had stood for over 300 years seemed to give up the fight for survival by falling in the severe October 1987 storm, barely two years after the closure of the institute.

In the Final Report of the NIRD there was a sad and pertinent comment:

'Successive Directors, administrators and research staff at the institute carried forward the work and responsibility believing that they were doing so in the long term interests of the institute, that is, the NIRD. It now seems that this is not to be. Most of those concerned will hope that the farms and facilities which they carefully developed will find a use for which they were intended whilst still retaining their public amenity value. It would be sad indeed, if this long stand of pleasant agricultural land following the River Loddon were allowed to deteriorate into haphazard redevelopment.'

To those of us who remember these former days, we now know such fears were indeed justified.

The Institute, as the giant cedar, is now a memory but will be a long fond memory to those in the village who have lived in a symbiotic relationship with it for so long.

So Long!

An Invitation

The company is situated on an industrial estate on the outskirts of Reading and produces scientific equipment for industrial use.

The firm was essentially divided between the 'below stairs' ie the laboratory where the products were prepared and tested and 'the above stairs' which housed the reception, sales, IT and marketing staff.

It was October in the final year of the millennium and my last exploit – the Grand National Draw earlier in the year had by now been forgotten.

It so happened that my annual selling of horses for the National draw had coincided with April 1st and with some assistance from my fellow conspirators, Nick and Mike, I had endeavoured to sell fictitious horse names to the unsuspecting staff.

Such well known horses as:

Got-no-hope,	Fat Chance,
Long Weigh Off,	Rear-view,
Unstable Condition	Falling Foru,
Fit to Drop,	Bitdown,
Tail to Tell,	Shortsleeve Jumper,
Bechers or Bust,	Gi' me Strength,
Suffolk Punch,	Upto Mischief,
Free Reign,	Rubdown

and   Off the Rails   were some examples.

We had successfully sold a dozen or so when one of the ladies called across the open-plan office 'Liz, I've drawn Had Me Oats, what have you got?'

'Thrush' came the reply.

This caused some degree of amusement and whilst further horse names were exchanged by the 'punters' we decided it was time to retreat from the office whilst we could still safely do so.

But it was now October and a young lady, Sylvia, had recently joined the laboratory staff and was discussing her recent invitation to the Ladies Christmas Party.

Now the company held a Christmas Dinner/Dance for all staff and their partners at a local hotel, but the ladies, who comprised about 60% of the workforce also organised their own additional function (strictly restricted to ladies and no partners).

This year it was to be a theme party 'Plunder the Pyramids' at Easthampstead Park Conference Centre in Wokingham.

On hearing Sylvia talking about her invitation I adventurously asked if she considered this just a trifle sexist and if she thought they might make an exception this year and invite me?

'No way!' she exclaimed 'you're a man', very much amused by the idea.

LADIES' CHRISTMAS PARTY

PLUNDER
THE PYRAMIDS

Ladies only—
no Partners

10th December

So this was a challenge. How do I go about getting an invitation to an all ladies function?

But time was on my side. With still a couple of months to go it allowed me a week or two to devise a strategy.

I discussed the challenge with Nick, my office colleague and drafted the following letter to be sent to Chris Burt, the company receptionist who was responsible for organising nearly all the Staff functions.

Easthampstead Park

Conference Centre

Wokingham

Berks. RG40 3DF

Our Ref: P/Pyramids 36-19

October 20th 1999

Dear Mrs Burt,

Re: Plunder the Pyramids

I have to inform you that we have been directed by Charlton Hotels, the group to which we are affiliated that their policy is to disallow single sex groups at Christmas and New Year functions. This is to conform to the 1998 Equal Rights & Sexual Discrimination Act 11 (a).

As manager of the Conference Centre I have to accept responsibility for the error made in accepting your booking for 10th December without notifying you of this change of policy. I trust that this early notification will enable you to rearrange your outing at an alternative venue.

A suggestion I can propose, and one some parties have accepted, is for you to consider including in your party at least one male member – this would enable Easthampstead Park to confirm your booking.

Mr Wass hopes to receive your menu selections in the next few days and I will hold your booking open at this stage to allow you to consider the available options.

I apologise once again for any inconvenience caused.

Yours sincerely,

R. D. Arling (Manager)

I posted it in Wokingham and awaited developments.

Two days later the letter arrived at reception and I was not prepared for the consternation it would unleash.

With the exception of the Managing Director and a couple of fellows in the IT department the remaining 'above stairs' staff were all ladies.

I ventured upstairs after the incoming mail had been opened to find a growing number of ladies surrounding Chris at reception and in deep and worried discussion. I returned to the laboratory a little concerned about how things would develop. Another half hour I made another sortie up to the open-plan office. The discussion group had grown.

This was worrying; I had no intention of bringing the whole of the 'above stairs' workforce to a grinding halt for a whole morning.

The Managing Director had emerged from his office a couple of times and although sympathetic to his ladies plight he was obviously not happy with the lack of industry.

Sue, one of the dozen or more ladies taking part in the discussion, caught me by the arm in passing and thrust the letter at me asking me what I thought.

I read it with a suitably furrowed brow and agreed, yes, it did pose a bit of a problem but suggested no solution.

Having retreated once again, I was increasingly concerned that it must be beginning to affect company turnover.

I couldn't let it continue. On returning once more to the office discussion group I was immediately grasped by the elbow and told that they had come to a decision. They were going to get a man to join them and would I agree to be the one?

Trying to suppress a smile and not wishing to raise suspicions by accepting too hastily, I broached the question of cost.

'Oh, don't you worry about that, we've all agreed to put in £3 or £4 each to cover it'.

A pang of guilt struck me.

How could I be so cruel to such nice generous ladies!

I asked to see the letter again as they all surrounded me.

'This seems quite interesting' I said, pointing to the bottom of the letter. 'Where it says ... Yours sincerely, R. D. Arling (Manager) there's a G and an R, I, N, D, A ...'

By the time I got to the L, I was half-way down the stairs followed by a harsh chorus of

'G R I N D A L.'

Although I kept a low profile for some time after this, I just knew that even if I was ever forgiven, this would never be forgotten.

A Lucky Break

March 2010 and I'd received the good news that I'd reached the final stage of the Sponsor's Customer Draw, open evidently to all those racegoers who had booked a corporate event at Newbury or Cheltenham Racecourse.

The prize was a 25% share in the racehorse, Amical Risks that was in training with Joss Saville. The draw was being run by BBH Marketing; a company responsible for horse racing promotions.

As I had had occasion to book a couple of boxes in the Berkshire Stand at Newbury recently, it appeared my name had been entered for this draw. And from visits to various racecourses over the years I was already aware that such shares is racehorses were offered through different organisations.

So it was not unusual. With luck you had the chance of winning a horse for a limited period with its keep and training fees already paid, and stabled with a recognised trainer.

So it seemed as though it was my lucky day.

However there was a slight niggle at the back of my mind.

As I was retiring from the firm in a couple of months I was a little suspicious. Could this be a wind-up from my work colleagues in response to the history of misdeeds laid at my door?

It needed some investigation so I went on-line.

Yes, Amical Risks was a French gelding with some races under its belt in France and which had subsequently been transferred to the UK.

It checked out that it had already run on the all-weather track at Wolverhampton and was indeed trained by Mr Joss Saville who was based at Middleham.

It all appeared to be authentic but to be absolutely certain I looked up the BBH Marketing web-site. That too existed.

All I was required to do was phone BBH Marketing and reply to some reference questions which I did.

I was to get my quarter share in Amical Risks and BBH said they would be in touch with me in due course.

May 1st, my retirement day had arrived. Mid-way through the morning I was called to the reception desk as an item had been delivered requiring my attention. I was presented with a set of vehicle ignition keys and directed to the front car park.

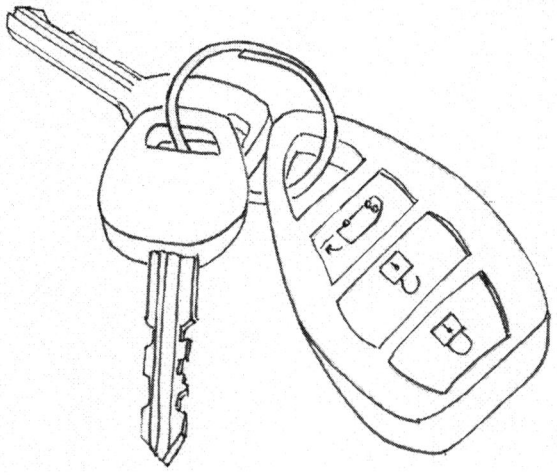

With some trepidation I arrived to discover a full-sized sparkling clean purple Lambourne Racehorse box with large printed plastic BBH Marketing banners on either side.

As I approached, it became increasingly evident that it was not empty!

The vehicle was rocking from side to side and there was a considerable noise emanating from within. There was loud whinnying and banging presumably from a rather upset animal.

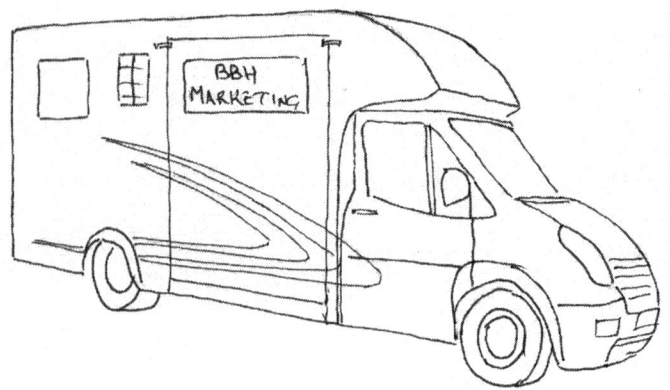

It was obviously unwise to open the rear doors but I noticed there was a small hatch that could be opened, situated halfway along the side of the wagon.

I gingerly opened the observation panel to discover four or five of the staff violently kicking the interior and rocking it to and fro.

The whinnying, I was to discover, was a recording blasting out from the driver's cab.

I later analysed the plan my colleagues had formulated.

(i)   Forming a viable plan.
(ii)   Writing the notification letter (headed notepaper and logos included).
(iii) Identifying a horse with a credible history and its current trainer.

(iv) Setting up a telephone number for my initial contact and manning the line.

(v) Creating a BBH Marketing web-site.

(vi) Booking a horsebox and driver.

(vii) Acquiring a recording of a whinnying horse.

(viii) Printing the BBH Marketing banners.

(ix) Organising all the staff and creating a timetable for the final day.

(x) Maintaining secrecy.

This was impressive, and could only have been achieved by Paula Johnson, her son Benjamin, and with her IT department capabilities, along with the co-operation of the whole workforce. Under different circumstances I would have been proud to have been part of such an organising committee.

I could only be extremely flattered that my colleagues had gone to such trouble and expense in planning this potentially risky enterprise and making my send off so very memorable.

... OR

was it RETRIBUTION for what had happened ten years previously? As Chris Burt and Sue Fidler were involved I guess it might be the latter.

' Two, Six, HEAVE'

(There was a thread in the Daily Telegraph newspaper letters' section, discussing the origin of the naval saying 'Two, Six, Heave' whenever anyone pulled on a rope. As my twin brother, Peter, had made a contribution, I thought I would add my tongue in cheek effort …)

Hoisting away

Sir- As Captain P. J. Grindal RN, (July 11th) has cast considerable doubt on Commander Langdon's theory (July 3rd) based on the gun-crew numbering system, I wish to add constructive comment to the origin of the expression "Two, Six, Heave!"

I understand the term to originate from the practice of rewarding ordinary seamen in the 17th & 18th centuries for carrying out some particularly strenuous chore like stepping new masts or mounting cannon.

2-6 refers to the cost of a firkin of ale; half a crown (or 2 shillings and sixpence) which was required to persuade the sailors of those days to do anything in unison.

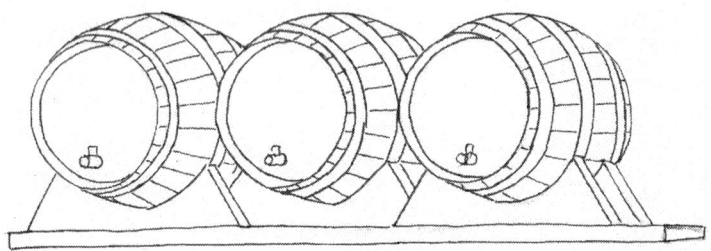

The practice was discontinued after 'bad ale' caused seamen, on an increasing number of occasions to 'heave' generally over the side or through the gun-ports.

Subsequently, "2-6-heave" became a derogatory comment on the beer sold in ale-houses and inns throughout the major seaports in England until the time of the Napoleonic Wars when rum contributed significantly to seamen's staple diet.

This practice has only relatively recently been discontinued, though, it should be stressed, not for the same reason.

I await with interest further comment on this subject and suggest that until such time this dietary explanation should be taken with more than a pinch of salt.

Yours faithfully,

Robert J. Grindal

National Institute for Research in Dairying, Shinfield, Reading.
RG2 9AT